ELEMENTS

Please visit our web site at: **www.garethstevens.com**
For a free color catalog describing Gareth Stevens Publishing's list of high-quality books and multimedia programs, call 1-800-542-2595 (USA) or 1-800-387-3178 (Canada). Gareth Stevens Publishing's fax: (414) 332-3567.

Library of Congress Cataloging-in-Publication Data

Elements.—North American ed.
      p. cm. — (Discovery Channel school science. physical science)
    "First published in 1999 as Stuff: the elements files by Discovery Enterprises, LLC, Bethesda, Maryland"—T.p. verso.
    Summary: Presents information and instructions for activities related to chemical elements found on Earth and in outer space.
    ISBN 0-8368-3357-0 (lib. bdg.)
    1. Chemical elements—Juvenile literature. [1. Chemical elements] I. Title.
II. Series.
QD466.E44   2003
546—dc21   2002030527

This edition first published in 2003 by
Gareth Stevens Publishing
A World Almanac Education Group Company
330 West Olive Street, Suite 100
Milwaukee, WI 53212 USA

This U.S. edition © 2003 by Gareth Stevens, Inc. First published in 1999 as *Stuff: The Elements Files* by Discovery Enterprises, LLC, Bethesda, Maryland. © 1999 by Discovery Communications, Inc.

Further resources for students and educators available at www.discoveryschool.com

Designed by Bill SMITH STUDIO
Creative Director: Ron Leighton
Design: Eric Hoffsten, Jay Jaffe, Brian Kobberger, Nick Stone, Sonia Gauba
Production Director: Peter Lindstrom
Photo Editor: Justine Price
Art Buyer: Lillie Caporlingua
Print consulting by Debbie Honig, Active Concepts
Gareth Stevens Editor: Betsy Rasmussen
Gareth Stevens Art Director: Tammy Gruenewald

Printed in the United States of America

1 2 3 4 5 6 7 8 9 07 06 05 04 03

Writers: David Krasnow, Tom Seddon

Editors: Jackie Ball, Bill Doyle

Photographs: p. 7, Pierre and Madam Curie, © Brown Brothers; pp. 4-5, computer chip, coal, iron object, © Alfred Pasieka/Science Photo Library; pp. 8-9, diamonds, © Alfred Pasieka/Science Photo Library; p. 15, Madam Curie, © Brown Brothers; pp. 16-17, helium balloon, © Alfred Pasieka/Science Photo Library; pp. 20-21, Hindenburg, © Brown Brothers; pp. 24-25, Las Vegas scene, © Brown Brothers.

Illustrations: pp. 16-17, map, Joe LeMonnier; pp. 28-29, boy with sandwich, Bob Bruger.

Acknowledgements: p. 15, excerpts from Madame Curie: A Biography by Eve Curie. Copyright © 1938 by Doubleday, Doran & Company, Inc. pp. 20-21, excerpts from The Periodic Table by Primo Levi. Copyright © 1984 by Schocken Books.

ELEMENTS

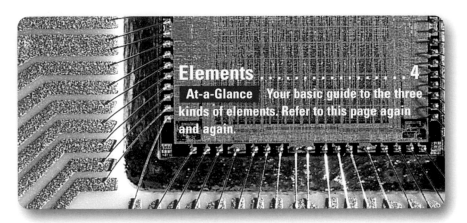

D on't look now, but you're covered with elements. Go ahead—try to brush them off. You'll have to brush pretty hard. Your clothes are made of elements. Your entire body is nothing but elements. So is the air you breathe and all the water, rock, and soil on Earth. These elements are almost always found as the building blocks of compounds and molecules.

Planets far away are made of the same elements as Earth, just put together a little differently. So what are they? What is this stuff? People have tried to answer that question for thousands of years. The ancient Chinese believed that water, earth, fire, metal, and wood were the five "elements" that made up all matter. Today we know that the Chinese count was on the low side. But you may be surprised to learn that only 115 to 118 elements exist and only 92 of those naturally occur on Earth. In fact, of those, just a handful makes up nearly all the matter in your body. But scientists keep finding more elements.

Read on as Discovery Channel shows you the *ELEMENTS* you and your world are made of.

You light up my life . . . See page 24

Final Project

3

Elements

Flake a bit of rust off the bumper of an old car. With the right equipment—like a chemistry set—you can break that rust into two elements, iron and oxygen. Nothing to it.

But now let's say you try to break those grains of iron into something else. Not so easy. In fact, impossible. No matter what you do to that iron, no matter what equipment you have, it's going to stay iron. That's what makes it an element. All you can do with elements is divide them into smaller and smaller pieces of themselves until you get to the smallest piece: an atom. How small is an atom? Trying to understand the size of an atom will boggle your mind. (For the record, it's about .0000000045 of an inch—.0001 micron—across.)

There are 115 known elements, and probably at least three more will be discovered soon. Chemists arrange them into three groups: metals, nonmetals, and metalloids.

BEWARE: METALLOIDS AHEAD

BEWARE: METALLOIDS AHEAD—These elements can't seem to make up their minds about what they are. They act like both metals and nonmetals, so they've been lumped into a category called metalloids. And it's a category you'd better handle with care. One metalloid, arsenic, poisoned quite a few kings in the Middle Ages. Selenium in the soil can kill livestock. (But selenium is also found in your body and in computer chips, where it gets along perfectly well. So go figure.)

IT'S A HARD LIFE: METALS

IT'S A HARD LIFE: METALS—Iron is an example of a metal—an especially strong one. As the major component of steel, it holds up tall buildings and is used to make cars, trains, and bikes. (Airplanes are mainly made of aluminum, which is lighter-weight.) In our blood, iron carries oxygen molecules to our cells. Like all metals, it has luster (shine) and conducts heat and electricity.

Like every metal except mercury, iron is a solid under normal conditions. (Mercury, the stuff in thermometers, will freeze, or turn solid, at -38° F or -38.88° C.

BABY, IT'S COAL OUTSIDE: NONMETALS

BABY, IT'S COAL OUTSIDE: NONMETALS—Metals might seem like the most useful group of elements, but life is mostly made of nonmetals. Take carbon, for example. About 18 percent, or one-sixth, of your body weight is carbon. And you're not alone. Every living thing contains this most elemental of the elements.

This lump of coal (below) is basically a lump of carbon. It once was a living thing, some decayed plant life from a swamp. After heating up and sitting under tons of rock for three hundred million years, all the hydrogen, oxygen, nitrogen, and other elements inside the plants were burned off, and the living thing became a lump of coal. Nonmetals are a big and varied category. They're found in nature as gases, liquids, and solids.

A piece of copper looks different from a piece of carbon. So you know elements look different on the outside. But they're different inside too, even though some things are the same from one to another:

Each atom of every element has a nucleus. Every nucleus has protons, which are heavy particles with a positive electrical charge. Every nucleus (except simple hydrogen) also has neutrons, particles as heavy as protons but with no electrical charge. Orbiting every nucleus are electrons, lightweight particles with a negative electrical charge. The electrons whoosh around the nucleus in masses called electron clouds.

So what makes elements different? It's a matter of quantity. Scientists classify elements according to atomic number and atomic weight.

Atomic number is the number of protons in the nucleus.
Atomic weight is the number of protons and neutrons in the nucleus.
Each element has a unique atomic number and you can't change it, no matter how hard you might try. Because if you did, you'd be making a different element. If you removed a proton from a beryllium atom, it wouldn't be beryllium anymore. It would be lithium, and it would act completely differently.

2	4.003
He	
Helium	

10	20.18
Ne	
Neon	

18	39.95

Al	**Si**	**P**	**S**	**Cl**	**Ar**
Aluminum	Silicon	Phosphorous	Sulfur	Chlorine	Argon

28	58.70	29	63.55	30	65.37	31	69.72	32	72.59	33	74.92	34	78.96	35	79.90	36	83.80
Ni		**Cu**		**Zn**		**Ga**		**Ge**		**As**		**Se**		**Br**		**Kr**	
Nickel		Copper		Zinc		Gallium		Germanium		Arsenic		Selenium		Bromine		Krypton	

46	106.40	47	107.87	48	112.41	49	114.82	50	118.69	51	121.75	52	127.60	53	126.90	54	131.30
Pd		**Ag**		**Cd**		**In**		**Sn**								**Xe**	
Palladium		Silver		Cadmium		Indium		Tin									

78	195.09	79	196.09	80	200.59	81	204.37	82	207.19	83							222
Pt																	
Platinum																	

110	269							285	115						293
Uum															**uo**
Unumilium															Ununoctium

COMPOUND INTEREST—Some elements exist on Earth as pure conglomerations of atoms, but the vast majority are found bound to or associated with other atoms in the form of compounds, ores, or molecules. Take chlorine. In nature, chlorine as an element is very rare; and yet, as a part of sodium chloride—sea salt—it is very common. As you read this book, pay particular attention to when the element exists all by itself or in association with other atoms.

THE SYMBOL TRUTH—Once upon a time, chemists in different countries called elements by different names. When they read one another's research, they could hardly keep anything straight. Then an organization, the International Union of Pure and Applied Chemistry, stepped in. IUPAC standardized the names of the elements and gave each a one- or two-letter code that stands for the name. O is oxygen, C is carbon. Some symbols were borrowed from Latin; Fe is the symbol for iron, which is called ferrum in Latin.

64	157.25	65	158.93	66	162.50	67	164.93	68	167.26	69	168.93	70	173.04	71	174.97
Gd		**Tb**		**Dy**		**Ho**		**Er**		**Tm**		**Yb**		**Lu**	

ELEMENTARY, MY

Easy for us to say what's an element and what's not. By now we have centuries of thinking and experiments behind us. But how did we come to understand the nature of matter?

About 3000 BC	About 600–300 BC	By AD 1000	Middle Ages (800s–1300s)	About 1674

Ancient cultures work with the first elements found in nature: gold, silver, and copper.

Greek philosopher Thales of Miletus arrives at a theory that all matter is made of water. At the time, no one thinks to prove ideas through experiments.

Empedocles, a Greek philosopher, sees the world as composed of four fundamental substances, or elements: earth, air, fire, and water. Aristotle adds a fifth element called *ether*, a perfect substance of which heaven is supposedly composed. People continue to believe in ether theory until the 19th century.

Chinese scientists identify five elements—water, earth, fire, metal, and wood. Experiments are conducted on the elements to discover the secret of eternal life. The experiments are unsuccessful, but they result in the invention of gunpowder, an explosive mixture of the elements potassium, nitrogen, sulphur, and carbon.

Islamic scientists and physicians develop alchemy, the idea of changing one element into another. Their method mixes experiment and magic. Books by Aga Khan, al-Razi (886–925), and Avicenna (980–1036) influence European alchemists, who become obsessed with changing lead into gold. Although this was (and is still) not possible, experiments by Roger Bacon and others pave the way for modern chemistry.

Looking for gold, Hennig Brand, an alchemist in Hamburg, Germany, lets many gallons of his own urine dry into a solid. He doesn't get gold (surprise). But he does discover the element phosphorus, which helps give urine its color.

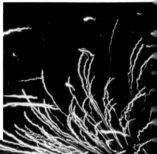

DEAR EMPEDOCLES

1789	About 1830	1869	1898–99	1996

Modern chemistry comes into being. French scientist Antoine Lavoisier publishes a textbook that includes much of what had been learned about the nature of matter up to the time. He defines *element* the same way we do now. His "Table of Simple Substances" lists 33 substances, some of which are later found to be compounds—combinations of elements—rather than pure elements.

John Dalton puts forth the theory that all matter is made up of atoms. He draws up a table of 20 elements and arrives at an atomic weight for each element. History will prove that many of his figures are very accurate.

The periodic table, including 65 elements, is published by Russian chemist Dmitri Mendeleev. We're still using essentially the same table today (see pages 8–9). His table predicts elements that have not been discovered yet, such as gallium and scandium. Mendeleev is even able to correctly describe these elements before anyone has seen them.

While researching the properties of uranium, Marie and Pierre Curie discover two new elements: radium and polonium. Their assistant discovers actinium. These are all radioactive elements—they give off rays and particles naturally and can transmute (change) into other elements. In 1903, they share the Nobel Prize for discovering radioactivity.

Physicists in Berkeley, CA, create element 118, which is given the name ununoctium from the International Union of Pure and Applied Chemistry.

Activity

COUNT 'EM UP How many elements can you think of? Start by making a careful list as you look around the items in your room or around your house or outside. Consider metals, metalloids, and nonmetals. Next to each, write what you know about each element (for instance, "iron is a hard metal"). Check your work by looking at the periodic table on pages 8 and 9. Were any of your "elements" not really elements?

Stack 'Em Up

1	1.01
H	
Hydrogen	

The chemist's most useful tool probably isn't the test tube or the bunsen burner. It's the periodic table of elements. It lists all the elements known in an order that tells us quite a few things about them. How did this table come to be?

Metals

Metalloids

Nonmetals

Lettering Color Codes:

Solids

Liquids

Gases

3	6.94	4	9.01
Li		**Be**	
Lithium		Beryllium	

11	22.99	12	24.31
Na		**Mg**	
Sodium		Magnesium	

19	39.10	20	40.08	21	44.96	22	47.90	23	50.94	24	51.996	25	54.94	26	55.85
K		**Ca**		**Sc**		**Ti**		**V**		**Cr**		**Mn**		**FE**	
Potassium		Calcium		Scandium		Titanium		Vanadium		Chromium		Manganese		Iron	

37	39.10	38	87.62	39	88.91	40	91.22	41	92.91	42	95.94	43	98	44	101.07
Rb		**Sr**		**Y**		**Zr**		**Nb**		**Mo**		**Tc**		**Ru**	
Rubidium		Strontium		Yttrium		Zirconium		Niobium		Molybdenum		Technetium		Ruthenium	

55	132.91	56	137.33	57	138.91	72	178.49	73	180.95	74	183.85	75	186.21	76	190.20
Cs		**Ba**		**La**		**Hf**		**Ta**		**W**		**Re**		**Os**	
Cesium		Barium		Lanthanum		Hafnium		Tantalum		Tungsten		Rhenium		Osmium	

87	223	88	226.03	89	227.03	104	261	105	262	106	266	107	264	108	269
Fr		**Ra**		**Ac**		**Rf**		**Ha**		**Sg**		**Bh**		**Hs**	
Francium		Radium		Actinium		Rutherfordium		Hahnium		Seaborgium		Bohrium		Hassium	

Atomic Number

26	55.85	— Atomic Weight
FE		— Symbol
Iron		— Name

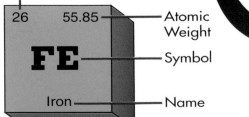

58	140.12	59	140.91	60	144.24	61	145	62	150.35
Ce		**Pr**		**Nd**		**Pm**		**Sm**	
Cerium		Praseodymium		Neodymium		Promethium		Samarium	

90	232.04	91	231.04	92	238.03	93	237.05	94	244
Th		**Pa**		**U**		**Np**		**Pu**	
Thorium		Protactinium		Uranium		Neptunium		Plutonium	

Chemist Dmitri Mendeleev arranges the elements. This table had been in the works for a thousand years. Mendeleev refines it by arranging the elements by atomic number: the number of protons in an element's nucleus. Elements that have the same number of electrons in their outer shells are arranged in vertical columns.

Why are the electron shells so important? Elements combine with other elements by sharing, losing, or gaining electrons. So the number of electrons in the outer shell determines how the element will behave with others. A helium atom, for example, has an outer shell of two electrons. It doesn't want to combine with any other atoms. It won't explode or react in some other dangerous way, which makes it a safe filler for a child's balloon. Lithium, on the other hand, has an outer shell with just one electron. It always wants to lose that electron, or to pick up a few more from somewhere else. It is a very reactive metal. Lithium is never found in nature on its own, but always as a compound.

					2 4.003 **He** Helium
5 10.81 **B** Boron	6 12.01 **C** Carbon	7 14.01 **N** Nitrogen	8 15.999 **O** Oxygen	9 18.998 **F** Fluorine	10 20.18 **Ne** Neon
13 26.98 **Al** Aluminum	14 28.09 **Si** Silicon	15 30.97 **P** Phosphorus	16 32.06 **S** Sulfur	17 35.45 **Cl** Chlorine	18 39.95 **Ar** Argon

27 58.93 **Co** Cobalt	28 58.70 **Ni** Nickel	29 63.55 **Cu** Copper	30 65.37 **Zn** Zinc	31 69.72 **Ga** Gallium	32 72.59 **Ge** Germanium	33 74.92 **As** Arsenic	34 78.96 **Se** Selenium	35 79.90 **Br** Bromine	36 83.80 **Kr** Krypton
45 102.91 **Rh** Rhodium	46 106.40 **Pd** Palladium	47 107.87 **Ag** Silver	48 112.41 **Cd** Cadmium	49 114.82 **In** Indium	50 118.69 **Sn** Tin	51 121.75 **Sb** Antimony	52 127.60 **Te** Tellurium	53 126.90 **I** Iodine	54 131.30 **Xe** Xenon
77 192.22 **Ir** Iridium	78 195.09 **Pt** Platinum	79 196.09 **Au** Gold	80 200.59 **Hg** Mercury	81 204.37 **Tl** Thallium	82 207.19 **Pb** Lead	83 208.98 **Bi** Bismuth	84 209 **Po** Polonium	85 210 **At** Astatine	86 222 **Rn** Radon
109 268 **Mt** Meitnerium	110 269 **Uum** Unumilium	111 272 **Uuu** Unununiium	112 277 **Uub** Ununbium	113 Not yet synthesized	114 285 **Uuq** Ununquadium	115 Not yet synthesized	116 289 **Uuh** Ununhexium	117 Not yet synthesized	118 293 **Uuo** Ununoctium

63 151.96 **Eu** Europium	64 157.25 **Gd** Gadolinium	65 158.93 **Tb** Terbium	66 162.50 **Dy** Dysprosium	67 164.93 **Ho** Holmium	68 167.26 **Er** Erbium	69 168.93 **Tm** Thulium	70 173.04 **Yb** Ytterbium	71 174.97 **Lu** Lutetium
95 243 **Am** Americium	96 247 **Cm** Curium	97 247 **Bk** Berkelium	98 251 **Cf** Californium	99 252 **Es** Einsteinium	100 257 **Fm** Fermium	101 258 **Md** Mendelevium	102 259 **No** Nobelium	103 262 **Lr** Lawrencium

NUMBER, PLEASE?

112	277
Uub	
Ununbium	

Q: You're Element 112—one of the new kids on the periodic table. What's your story?

A: I was born at the Heavy-Ion Research Center in Darmstadt, Germany, in February 1996. Elements 110 and 111 were discovered there, too. So I guess you could call us siblings.

Q: What do you mean, you were born? Aren't elements found in nature? You know, there from the beginning?

A: Nope. Didn't you read page 2? Only the elements up to Number 92 are natural. The rest of us—the heaviest ones—were created. Or, as I prefer to say, synthesized.

Q: Wild. So what's it like to be synthesized?

A: Well, I don't remember much, but I'm told that scientists bombarded lead, atomic number 82, with a high-energy beam of zinc, atomic number 30.

Q: So why do they call you 112?

A: You're kidding, right? Here's a giant hint. The atomic number for lead is 82, for 82 protons in the nucleus. The atomic number for zinc is 30, for 30 protons.

Q: OK. So?

A: So, do the math! What's 82 plus 30?

Q: Oh, I get it—112. Cool.

A: Yeah, isn't it?

Q: But don't you get sick of being called by a number? Do you think you'll ever get a real name to replace that silly "un" name, which just means "one, one, two" in Latin? You know, like tin or germanium or something?

A: Oh, sure, but I can't say when. There's a little backlog at the International Union of Pure and Applied Chemistry in Geneva, Switzerland, where the naming gets done.

Q: Well, what would you like your name to be?

A: Haven't thought about it much. I kind of like Samarium, or Sam for short, but that's taken by Number 62. And Molybdenum's kind of neat, too, but that's taken by number 42. Or maybe Marienium, after my hero, Marie Curie. Say, I think we should speed up the pace a little here.

Q: Why?

A: Because I'm only around for a fraction of a second and then I split up.

Q: Huh?

A: I'm unstable. Friends have suggested therapy, but it's just my nature.

Q: Why are you unstable?

A: Well, 112 is a high atomic number. That's a lot of protons in one nucleus. Too many, if you ask me. Which you did. And you know what happens when there are too many protons.

Q: No, what?

A: They find it hard to stay put. I lose them all the time. They decay into other elements. It happens to a lot of us. All the elements with atomic numbers higher than uranium decay at different rates.

Q: That's a shame!

A: Yeah, well—no use crying over spilled protons.

Q: Just a few more questions. Being made in a lab, do you ever feel inferior to the natural elements?

A: Nah. Why should I? Take hydrogen and helium, which form in the sun. Protons are bashed together under intense heat to form their nuclei. That's not so different from the way the Darmstadt folks made me. In bigger, much hotter stars, heavier elements like carbon, oxygen, nitrogen, neon, and magnesium are formed like hydrogen and helium too. So how is that better than old 112?

Q: I guess you have a point. But if you could stick around longer, what would you do with your time?

A: I'd like to check out a supernova—the catastrophic explosion of a collapsing star. You talk about heavy! That's where all the heavy elements in our solar system, from iron up to uranium, form. They've drifted here over the history of the universe. A supernova—yep, that would be a sight to see. But there's no point wishing. Decay is just a fact of life for a radioactive element like me. Gotta go.

Activity

ASKED AND ANSWERED What questions would you ask an element? Which element, and why? Write an interview of your own. Do some research to come up with the best answers you can.

Who's Got Gas?

SCRAPBOOK

Earth has gas. Big time. But don't worry—most of the elements that occur as gases aren't stinky. Gas is one of three states of matter. The others are solids and liquids. Only a handful of the elements are found in nature in the form of gases, although almost any element can become a gas if it is made hot enough. An element in a gaseous state does not have a definite shape or volume. A gas will fill any container it is put in. What else is so special about gas?

Leave Me Alone!

Helium, neon, argon, krypton, xenon, and radon are classed as inert gases, but they have another name, too: the noble gases. You could also call them snob gases. They don't want to hang out with any other elements. Are they too cool, or maybe just shy? Actually, what they are is fed up—with electrons. These gases have complete electron shells, so they have no electrons to share with other elements. They don't combine. They don't normally form compounds. They just float by themselves.

OH, O!

Oxygen is the element we have a lot of. Good thing, because with just a little less of it in the air, you'd pass out. About one-fifth of the atmosphere is oxygen, found as the molecule O_2. Nearly two-thirds of the weight of your body is oxygen, too. So why don't you float like a balloon? Because most of your body's oxygen is tied up in a compound— a compound that consists of two hydrogen atoms and one oxygen atom. Chemists write its formula as H_2O. Sound familiar? You got it. Water. The wet stuff is the stuff YOU are mostly made of. Knowing that, it may sound funny that oxygen supports burning. But it does. So can hydrogen. In fact, our air would explode if nitrogen didn't balance things out. But when you put hydrogen and oxygen together, you have the substance that puts OUT fires. Many compounds are like that—totally unlike the elements they are made from.

What a Dump!

Ever walk past a garbage dump and smell something a little . . . funny? All living things contain carbon, and when they die and decay, they generally release a gas called methane. A methane molecule is composed of one carbon and four hydrogen atoms. But don't turn up your nose at methane. One day it might carry you far—in a car or a bus, for example. It's the main component of a substance called natural gas. Like oil, natural gas is a good source of energy because it burns, and that releases energy. It makes less pollution than gasoline. Already some buses are powered by natural gas. The stuff is so useful that landfills, built of garbage, have systems of pipes to collect the methane that forms deep in the heap.

That's a Wrap

The atmosphere is a 50-mile-thick (80 km) layer of gases surrounding Earth that protects Earth from the cold void out there. For comparison, jet planes usually fly at about 7 miles (11 km) high. Without the atmosphere, we would need the same gear astronauts use in space. Any planet large enough to have strong gravity will hold an atmosphere.

What elements make up Earth's protective wrapper? Mostly nitrogen as N_2 (78.09%) and oxygen as O_2 (20.95%). Argon, an inert gas, makes up just under one percent, and the compound carbon dioxide contributes 0.03%. After that, we have traces of neon, helium, krypton (yes, THAT krypton), and hydrogen.

Activity

MAKE YOUR OWN SCRAPBOOK

It doesn't have to just include gases. You could collect images and descriptions of one or more of your favorite elements in action. Attach some souvenirs! What would someone reading your scrapbook learn about you from it?

ALL AGLOW

Paris, France, 1897

Marie Sklodovska Curie was a young physicist struggling to take care of a baby daughter, teach chemistry at a high school, and complete her research to earn the French equivalent of our Ph.D. She had moved to France from Poland to get her education in one of Europe's finest universities, the Sorbonne, and there she had met and married another scientist, Pierre Curie.

For her degree, Marie Curie decided to follow up on an observation made by another scientist, Henri Becquerel. Becquerel had discovered that a compound—a combination of two elements—containing uranium seemed to give off rays of energy. No one knew how to account for this, and Marie Curie was curious to find out. She couldn't have guessed the revolutionary discovery that was at the end of that curiosity.

To conduct her studies, Curie set out to get uranium from a rock called pitchblende. The pure element uranium gave off energy, all right. Curie called it radioactive. But it turned out that raw pitchblende was far more radioactive than pure uranium. Her husband, Pierre Curie, a noted scientist, joined her in the task of identifying the mysterious substance that made it so radioactive, and the two set to work in a cold, drafty old shed.

"We had no money, no laboratory, and no help in the conduct of this important and difficult task. It was like creating something out of nothing. I may say without exaggeration that this period was, for my husband and myself, the heroic period of our common existence."

"And yet it was in this miserable old shed that the best and happiest years of our life were spent, entirely consecrated to work. I sometimes passed the whole day stirring a mass in ebullition [violent bubbling], with an iron rod nearly as big as myself. In the evening I was broken with fatigue."

Based on their findings, the Curies named two new elements: polonium (which was named after Marie's home country of Poland) and radium, which gave off an enormous amount of rays. But concluding that radium existed and getting a sample of it were very different things. Radium was so rare that Marie Curie, mostly on her own, processed eight thousand pounds of pitchblende ore to get a sample that would fit on her thumbnail.

The pure sample of radium had amazing properties. The energy it gave off glowed, a property called luminosity:

"This luminosity cannot be seen by daylight, but it can be easily seen in half darkness. The light emitted can be strong enough to read by, using a little of the product for light in darkness."

For some time, radium was used in a paint for watches that glowed in the dark. Even more amazing, radium made other objects radioactive, by causing the nuclei of other elements to become unstable. This caused great problems in the laboratory. How could the Curies measure radioactivity if their equipment was radioactive?

"When one studies strongly radioactive substances, special precautions must be taken if one wishes to be able to continue taking delicate measurements. The various objects used in a chemical laboratory, and those which serve for experiments in physics, all

14

become radioactive in a short time and act upon photographic plates through black paper. Dust, the air of the room, and one's clothes, all become radioactive. The air in the room is a conductor. In the laboratory where we work, the evil has reached an acute stage, and we can no longer have any apparatus completely isolated."

The Curies discovered both the hazards and the promises of radioactivity. They and Becquerel had both noticed minor burns where their fingers touched test tubes containing the element. Pierre Curie bravely placed radium on his arm to observe what would happen:

"After the action of the rays, the skin became red over a surface of six square centimeters; the appearance was that of a burn, but the skin was not painful, or barely so. At the end of several days the redness, without growing larger, began to increase in intensity; on the twentieth day it formed scabs, and then a wound which was dressed with bandages; on the forty-second day, the epidermis [skin] began to form again on the edges, working toward the center, and fifty-two days after the action of the rays there is still a surface of one square centimeter in the condition of a wound, which assumes a grayish appearance indicating deeper mortification."

Radium, or rather radioactivity, destroys human tissue. Doctors quickly sought ways to use small doses of radiation to destroy diseased cells, or tumors. The Curies used their sample of radium for this purpose and took a strong interest in the efforts of other doctors in the field of medicine called radiology. Radiation still serves today as one of the principal ways to treat cancer.

The radioactivity that the Curies discovered, however, proved to be as dangerous as it was helpful. Marie Curie had a long illness and died from leukemia, a form of cancer that was probably caused by her unprotected exposure to radiation.

Activity

ATOMIC CONFLICT Medicine isn't the only beneficial use of radiation. Nuclear power uses the energy from the radioactive elements uranium or plutonium to create electricity for human use. Nuclear power needs only small amounts of uranium to work, and it does not pollute the environment the way burning coal or oil does. But it produces wastes that will remain radioactive, and therefore dangerous to living things, for many thousands of years. Debate the use of nuclear energy. Is it a sensible alternative or a dangerous mistake?

Treasure Hunt

Is there a hunk of silver just sitting in your backyard? Check this map to find out! It shows the location of major deposits of ten elements. Many of these elements are found in rocks called ores.

Coal

Copper

Diamonds

Gold

Iron

Lead

Platinum

Silver

Tin

Uranium

Activity

SAVE THE WORLD!

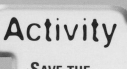

Dear Humans:
You must provide us with large quantities of any two of the following elements:

- Platinum
- Gold
- Uranium
- Silver

Deliver by this time tomorrow or we will destroy your planet. We appreciate your cooperation.

Sincerely,
Space Aliens

This time tomorrow? You'll only have time to make it to two continents. Which two continents will give you the most of which two elements?

Where are you going to find the stuff to prevent our planet's doom?

AMAZING BUT TRUE

You Precious Things

Gold. Diamonds. Glittering, gleaming, highly prized, highly priced. Two of the most precious substances on Earth. And here's something else the two have in common: they're both elements.

You're probably not surprised that gold is an element—after all, it is a metal—but diamonds? You won't find them on the periodic table. But a diamond is an element all the same. It's what happens when you take a lump of the element carbon and bury it for millions of years under tons of pressure.

Dazzling, but Dangerous?

Carbon exists in more than one form. Graphite is a soft, black form. A diamond is a hard, colorless form. In fact, a diamond is the hardest substance found in nature, taking its strength from the very tight arrangement between carbon atoms. Diamonds can cut glass, which is why the lowest quality stones are used as cutting tools. Gem diamonds, the kinds in beautiful jewelry, were first found in streambeds in India and Borneo. Many now come from South Africa and can also be found in Australia, Russia, and Angola.

Two of the most famous diamonds are the Koh-I-Noor, now among the English crown jewels, and the Cullinan, from which 105 individual stones were cut. But the most famous is the Hope Diamond. Or, some might say, infamous. Read on and decide for yourself.

Paris, France, 1668

French merchant named Jean Baptiste Tavernier brings a 112-carat (22,400 mg) blue diamond from India to France. Legend has it that the gem is cursed because a thief stole it long ago from the eye of a statue of the Hindu goddess Sita. Tavernier sells the diamond to King Louis XIV, who has it cut into a 67-carat heart-shaped stone and names it the Blue Diamond of the Crown. On his next trip to India, the story goes, Tavernier is killed by wild dogs.

King Louis XVI and Queen Marie Antoinette inherit the "French Blue." In 1792, at the height of the French Revolution, it is stolen along with all the other French crown jewels. The king and queen lose their heads at the guillotine, and the diamond supposedly makes its way to Wilhelm Fals, a Dutch diamond cutter. Fals recuts it—and his son steals it from him. The father dies of grief over the theft. The son commits suicide.

In 1830, Henry Hope buys a 44.5-carat deep blue oval-cut diamond that gem experts agree is the French Blue. It becomes known as the Hope Diamond; over the next eighty years, at least three owners meet with tragedy. In 1911, a wealthy and eccentric American socialite named Evalyn Walsh McLean purchases it. Later her son is killed in a car crash; her husband dies in a mental hospital; and her daughter dies of an overdose of sleeping pills.

Mrs. McLean dies (of natural causes), and New York jeweler Harry Winston purchases all her jewels in 1947. Eleven years later, he gives the stone to the Smithsonian Institute in Washington, D.C., where it is on permanent display. He may have been glad to get rid of it.

All That Glitters

Gold has been prized and used by humans since prehistoric times. It may be the very first metal people ever used. Gold is a soft metal; in fact, it's typically hardened by other metals to make it useable. It also often occurs in nature as an alloy—a mixture of metals.

The gold content of an alloy is stated in carats. Solid gold is 24 carats. Eighteen-carat "gold" is actually only three-quarters gold, with the rest made of some other metal. Gold can be found in the form of dust, grains, flakes, or nuggets and occurs in quartz veins or lodes, usually in deposits. The majority of the world's supply comes from South Africa; but there's gold in the U.S., too, in South Dakota and Nevada.

How much gold is there in the world? Not a lot. In fact, some people say that all the gold refined since we started keeping track of it could be placed in a single cube 60 feet (18 m) on each side. Picture a blocky, yellow six-story apartment building.

One of gold's most fascinating properties is its malleability. That means it can be hammered thin—so thin that a single ounce could be pounded out to a sheet big enough to carpet a room or two of your house.

At one time, gold could be extracted by panning it from a stream, but most of these sources are practically used up. Today, we get gold by crushing ore to a powder to expose the small gold particles, then using a chemical process. But gold still has the same powerful appeal it's had for centuries.

Northern South America, Around 1530

A fabulous country full of gold is rumored to exist somewhere in South America. The country is called El Dorado, which means "gilded one," after its king. This ruler is supposedly so rich that he powders his body with gold dust each day and washes it off in a lake at night, while his subjects throw offerings of jewels and more gold into the water. (Today we think the legend probably started with the Chibcha Indians, who lived around present-day Bogota, Colombia, and were said to practice a similar ritual.)

Eager to find this treasure trove, Spanish conquistadores and European explorers launch expeditions through much of northern South America. Native peoples are enslaved or killed in the process. The last exploration, led by Sir Walter Raleigh, takes place in 1617. When he fails to bring back gold, Raleigh is executed. El Dorado is never found, but the search results in the exploration of Venezuela, Colombia, Chile, and Ecuador—as well as the loss of many lives through starvation, disease, and other hardships.

Activity

OF CURSE NOT Stories and legends are one thing; facts and proof are another. How would you go about proving or disproving that there is a curse on the Hope Diamond? Design an investigation into the matter, raising questions and gathering as many facts as you can.

Mine, All Mine

EYEWITNESS ACCOUNT

California, 1849

Seeking instant riches, thousands swarm into the hills of California to sift dirt in streams, going for the gold. Because gold is heavier than most common elements, all it takes is swishing a pan of dirt around to separate the lighter elements. But "all" means standing waist deep in a freezing cold stream for ten hours a day. Not an easy way to get rich. But sometimes panning pays off with nuggets weighing several ounces. The chance of easy gold brings so many hopeful diggers to California that its gold fields are practically exhausted in about three years.

Turin, Italy, about 1942

Those few lucky forty-niners who found gold were the exception. Most elements don't exist by themselves in nature. They're found in compounds. Chemists figure out how to break apart these compounds to purify the elements they want. Other elements are found buried in masses of rock that may contain many other elements.

In about 1942, Primo Levi was a young chemist just out of school and looking for a job. He found one, but it was a tough one: to come up with a way to get nickel out of a gigantic heap of waste rock from an asbestos mine. In his own words:

All mines are magical per se, and always have been. The entrails [guts] of the earth swarm with gnomes … who can be generous and let you find a treasure beneath the tip of your pickax, or deceive and bedazzle you, making modest pyrites glitter like gold, or disguising zinc in the garb of tin; and, in fact, many are the minerals whose names have roots that signify "deception, fraud, bedazzlement."

This mine too had its magic, its wild enchantment. On a squat, bleak hill, all jagged rocks and stumps, was sunk a cone-shaped gorge, an artificial crater, four hundred meters [1,300 feet] in diameter: it was in every way similar to the schematic representations of Hell in Dante's Divine Comedy. Along the encircling tiers, day by day, were exploded dynamite charges; the material shaken loose would roll down to the bottom but without gaining too much speed.

The plant was built in a tier along the slope of the hill and beneath the tunnel's opening; in it the mineral was shattered in a huge crusher that the director described to me and demonstrated with almost childlike enthusiasm. It was a bell turned upside down, four meters [13 feet] in diameter and constructed of massive steel; at its center, suspended from above and guided from below, swung a gigantic clapper. The oscillation [vibration] was slight, barely visible, but was enough to split in the blink of an eye the mass of rock pressed together lower down . . . [which] split again, and came out from below in fragments as large as a man's head. The operation proceeded in the midst of an apocalyptic uproar, a cloud of dust which could be seen down on the plain. The material was crushed again until it became

gravel, then dried out and sifted; and it wasn't difficult to figure out that the final purpose of this gigantic labor was to extract a miserable 2 percent of asbestos which was trapped in those rocks. All the rest, thousands of tons a day, was dumped at random in the valley.

I fell in love with my work from the very first day, although it entailed nothing more at that stage than quantitative analysis of rock samples: attack with hydrofluoric acid, down comes iron with ammonia, down comes nickel (how little! a pinch of red sediment) with dimethylglyoxime, down comes magnesium with phosphate, always the same, every blessed day—in itself, it was not very stimulating. But stimulating and new was another sensation: the sample to be analyzed was no longer an anonymous, manufactured powder, a quiz: it was a piece of rock, the earth's entrail, torn from the earth by the explosive's force.

Activity

DOWN AND DIRTY You probably don't have a heap of mining waste, known as slag, handy. But you may be surprised at how many different materials you can find if you analyze sand, gravel, or soil. Bring in a cupful from the schoolyard or someplace near your home. Use a magnifying glass to study the sample, separating the different groups of material by eye. Name each group ("pinkish sand," "brown dirt," "twigs"). Calculate approximately what fraction of the whole each group represents. And please—wash your hands when you're done.

21

Trouble in the Air

The passengers were crowded around the large windows of the lounges, watching the ground grow closer by the inch. "It takes so long to come down," said Emma. "Can't the captain make it go quicker?" Storms and lightning had delayed the airship's arrival, and now landing seemed to take forever.

The little girl fidgeted with impatience. She had been on the big airship for over three days, and the excitement and terror of floating far above the Atlantic Ocean had finally worn off. Her mother explained for the tenth time how the craft was held up by hydrogen, which

was lighter than air. That's why it floated. In order to land, the ship had to slowly let out some gas so that it became heavier than air again. But all Emma could think about now was seeing her American cousins for the summer. They would be so jealous of her trip in the airship.

At 804 feet (245 m), the airship was the largest aircraft ever flown. Unlike floppy "blimps" filled with helium, this was a zepellin, an airship with a metal frame. The metal added weight, so it had tanks filled with hydrogen. Hydrogen was lighter than helium and could carry more weight. The tanks were covered with fabric that was reinforced with aluminum.

Emma's father came out of the smoking lounge. He had been complaining the whole trip about having to smoke in this one cramped room, which had been specially designed to make sure none of the airship's gas could leak in. And he and the other passengers had to light cigars from a special electric lighter that would not spark. Emma's father looked a little nervous, because he had seen lightning in the distance, but he didn't want to mention anything to his wife and daughter. He sat down at the airship's baby grand piano and began to play the national anthem in honor of their arrival in the United States.

"Why, just look at this!" Emma's mother called. "Cables are being lowered from the ship. There, you can see those workers attaching them to that metal mast on the ground. It must be too windy for us to set down gently."

"We must be in for a bumpy landing," remarked her father. Then the tone of his voice changed suddenly. "What was that? It felt like we hit something!"

The ship was only two hundred feet off the ground when something went wrong. Eyewitnesses reported seeing a glow around the ship as though the air were charged with electricity. Then there was a booming sound, and the rear of the aircraft was on fire. Emma and her family were among the lucky ones—they escaped through the front of the craft. What were the possible causes of the crash? Look through the clues and then try to figure it out. (Answer is on page 32.)

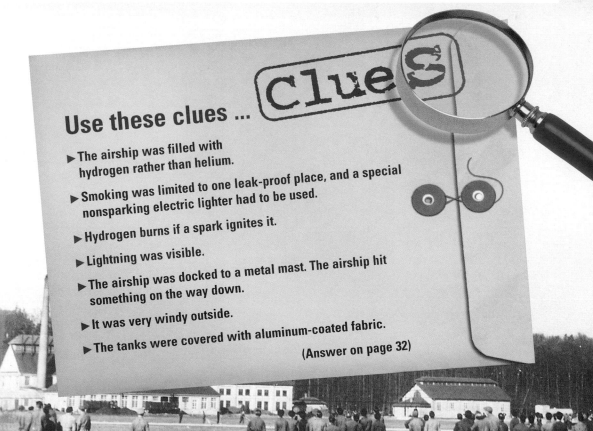

Use these clues ... Clues

- ▶ The airship was filled with hydrogen rather than helium.
- ▶ Smoking was limited to one leak-proof place, and a special nonsparking electric lighter had to be used.
- ▶ Hydrogen burns if a spark ignites it.
- ▶ Lightning was visible.
- ▶ The airship was docked to a metal mast. The airship hit something on the way down.
- ▶ It was very windy outside.
- ▶ The tanks were covered with aluminum-coated fabric.

(Answer on page 32)

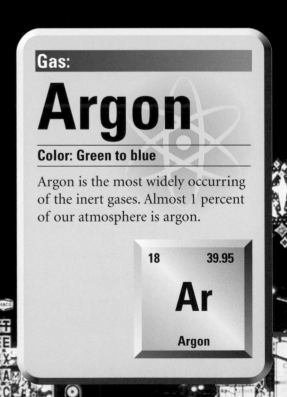

The Light Stuff

How can you tell one clear, odorless gas from another? A common method is to run some tests by combining the gas with other elements to see what compounds form. (Chemists call this method of identifying elements qualitative analysis.)

But what if compounds are very difficult to form? Try putting the element in a vacuum—a container empty of everything, including air—and then putting an electrode at each end, like a battery. If the electricity causes the gas to light up, you might have an inert gas on your hands.

Not to mention a special kind of art form.

Gas:

Neon

Color: Reddish orange

Neon was the first inert gas used in lighting. We generally call these fixtures "neon lights," even when they are made with other gases—which they often are in order to get a certain color. Commercial signs typically contain a coating of mercury on the inside of the glass tube, which affects the color. The glass used to make the tube may also be colored by mixing it with a metallic compound. Craftspeople can bend the glass tubes containing the gases into almost any shape.

10	20.18
Ne	
Neon	

Gas:

Argon

Color: Green to blue

Argon is the most widely occurring of the inert gases. Almost 1 percent of our atmosphere is argon.

18	39.95
Ar	
Argon	

Gas:

Xenon
(ZEE non)

Color: Blue

When Canadian chemist Neil Bartlett created a compound from inert xenon, the feat was considered so amazing that he won the Nobel Prize.

54	131.30
Xe	
Xenon	

Gas:

Krypton

Colorless

Krypton is mixed with argon in fluorescent lights. Fluorescent lights are much more efficient than regular light bulbs with filaments, which are known as incandescents. Incandescents heat up more, which wastes energy. But fluorescents are cooler and last longer because there's no filament to burn up with a sizzle—that familiar "POP" that means the bulb has burned out.

36	83.80
Kr	
Krypton	

Blast Back to the Beginning

Where do all these elements come from? That's what scientists would like to find out. We do know that the Sun is like a gigantic factory for hydrogen and helium. It makes these two elements—the lightest ones in the periodic table, having atomic numbers 1 and 2 respectively—from protons and electrons that whiz around inside it at nearly the speed of light. In this nuclear reaction, a great deal of energy is released—so much that the Sun's energy reaches Pluto, 3.66 billion miles (5.89 billion km) away.

But hydrogen and helium are only two of the 92 natural elements known. The other 90 must have formed some other way. Don Burnett is the Lead Scientist at NASA for a project called Genesis. This word means "beginnings," and that's what Burnett and his colleagues are after.

"The benefit to scientists will be to help understand the way our Solar System formed," Burnett explains. "What the input materials were, what events took place to form planetary materials, and what processes took place during these events."

Those events took place billions of years ago. Genesis launched a spacecraft in January 2001 that traveled a million miles (1.6 million km) toward the Sun. That's still some 92 million miles (148 million km) from the glowing gas furnace, but it's a start. That distance will keep it out of Earth's magnetic field, so that matter being drawn to our planet doesn't get into its collectors. The craft is "sunbathing." With open collectors, it gathers waves of matter called solar winds. Later, it will return to Earth with its cargo, and scientists will get to work finding out what those winds are made of.

"We all assume that the Sun and the planets formed from the same cloud of gas and dust," Burnett remarks. "But the Sun and the planets are very different, and all the planets are different from one another. Why? Many things must have happened with this cloud of gas and dust to create all this diversity. The Sun is a ball of gas; Earth is a rock. This is a big difference in composition. If it had been real cold when Earth formed, many of the volatile (unstable) materials in the Sun would have been retained. So it was hot when Earth formed, and most materials less volatile than rock were lost. Comparing differences like these yields interesting conclusions."

How does the *Genesis* spacecraft work? "This isn't quite like sending a robot out to pick up rocks," comments Eileen Stansbery, the Contamination Control Lead for the Genesis project. It's her job to make sure that the solar material doesn't get contaminated by other matter, or ruined as it is returned in the spacecraft. "We are letting ultraclean material literally sunbathe for a couple of years while atoms from the Sun embed themselves in the material, sort of like hiding themselves in a box. Those embedded atoms are our sample."

The origins of the universe might not change what you do tomorrow, but it could change how everybody understands the universe. After all, people once thought Earth was flat. "This is an example of fundamental research," says Burnett. "We won't make any direct changes in most people's lives, but greater under-standing of our origins should make everyone's life more satisfying. This is one aspect of being part of an 'advanced society'."

Elemental Employment

Want to work with elements? Brush up on your people skills. Most work is done in teams, where brainstorming and sharing information obtained through research is key.

Many U.S. **chemists** work in the petroleum, medicine, and food industries, spending most of their time in the lab or at a computer, analyzing data. Employers look for people with a degree in chemistry or a background in biology, but English and communications skills are important too. Watch the movie *Lorenzo's Oil* for inspiration.

Chemical engineers use their skills in everything from patent law to perfume-making. A few have even become astronauts. Or if you're equal parts artist and scientist, you may want to work with gems and metals. Some technical schools offer courses in stone setting, casting, and enameling.

Or take some courses in **horology**, the study of time and timekeepers, and become skilled in watchmaking, clock repair, engraving, and jewelry design and repair.

Activity

GET A JOB Write a help-wanted ad describing a position with the Genesis project. What educational background would a job like Don Burnett's or Eileen Stansbery's require? What are some of the duties? What personal qualities would help someone succeed? Would YOU want the job? Exchange job descriptions with a partner and write a letter asking for an interview. Don't forget to say "Thank you for your attention."

Eat Your Elements!

Looking for elements in the world around you? They're as near as your next meal. Look inside your lunch for a display of elements that keep you fine-tuned. Remember that most of these elements exist in association with other atoms as compounds or molecules.

SODIUM
sources: table salt, most foods and water
what it does: transmission of nerve impulses, internal water balance
not enough: muscle cramps, nausea, diarrhea
too much: high blood pressure in some people

PHOSPHORUS
sources: meat, poultry, fish, eggs, peas and beans, milk products
what it does: strong bones and teeth, energy release from nutrients
not enough: appetite loss, fatigue
too much: calcium deficiency

IODINE
sources: seafood, sea salt, iodized salt
what it does: thyroid gland function (produces hormones)
not enough: goiter (enlarged thyroid)
too much: goiter

ZINC
sources: meat, liver, eggs, poultry, seafood, milk, whole grains
what it does: enzyme formation (to digest food)
not enough: slow wound healing, loss of taste, stunted growth in children
too much: nausea, vomiting, anemia, stomach bleeding

Tuna, leafy lettuce, salt, whole-grain wheat bread

FLUORIDE
sources: fish, animal foods, fluoridated water
what it does: strong teeth, bones
not enough: dental decay
too much: discoloring of teeth, toxic in large doses

MAGNESIUM
sources: raw green leafy vegetables, nuts, seeds, whole grains
what it does: high energy muscle function
not enough: muscle weakness, irregular heartbeat
too much: disorders in nervous system

CALCIUM
sources: milk products, fish, dark green leafy vegetables, citrus fruits, beans
what it does: strong teeth and bones, blood clotting
not enough: rickets in children (bowed legs, stunted growth), osteoporosis in adults
too much: calcium deposits in body tissues, fatigue

IRON
sources: red meat, egg yolk, leafy vegetables, beans, molasses, whole grains
what it does: formation of red blood cells
not enough: anemia, fatigue
too much: toxic build-up in liver, pancreas, heart

You

Activity

LUNCH LOG What elements did you have for lunch today? Save the ingredient list of anything you ate that came in a wrapper or container, or use the information above for hints about unwrapped foods. Which elements are at work in your body now? Try it for a week. Which days gave you the biggest varieties of elements? Did you notice anything different about how you felt or acted on those days?

29

Let Me Atom

Cut It Out!

Do you have a pair of scissors? Then you may have what it takes to cut a piece of paper down to one atom.

What you will need:
- ▶ A strip of paper 11 inches (28 cm) long
- ▶ Scissors

What you do:
1. Cut the strip of paper in half.
2. Cut one of the halves into two more halves.
3. Keep cutting one of the halves into halves. Keep track of how many cuts you have made.
4. Watch your fingers! That paper's getting small already!
5. How many cuts did you make? Did you get down to atomic size?

This chart shows your progress.

Cut 1: 5.5 inches (14.0 cm)—size of a child's hand

Cut 2: 2.75 inches (7.0 cm)—fingers, ears, toes

Cut 3: 1.38 inches (3.5 cm)—face of a watch, mushroom, eye

Cut 4: .69 inches (1.75 cm)—keyboard keys, rings, bee

Cut 6: .17 inches (.43 cm)—sesame seeds

Cut 8: .04 inches (1 mm)—width of thread; congrats if you're still cutting

Cut 10: .01 inches (.25 mm)—most people have quit by now

Cut 12: .006 inches (.015 mm)—width of paper, microchip components

Cut 14: .002 inches (.05 mm)—microscopic range, human hair

Cut 18: .0004 inches (1 micron)—water purification openings, bacteria

Cut 19: .00018 inches (.5 micron)—waves of visible light

Cut 24: .0000006 inches (.0015 micron)—electron microscope range, cellular membranes

Cut 28: .0000000045 inches (.0001 micron)—size of an atom!

Okay, we cheated. What was your hint? Paper isn't an element, so there's no such thing as an atom of paper. But you get the point. Atoms are small.

Atomic Humor

Ellie: What did iron say when his kids left for school?

Nellie: I zinc they argon.

Neutron: How much to enter this nucleus?

Proton: For you, no charge.

Bk
Berkelium

Name Game

Ytterbium was named after Yhtterby, a village in Sweden where many unusual compounds have been found. In fact, three other elements—erbium, terbium, and yttruim—have been named after Ytterby.

26   55.85
Fe
Iron

Some elements are named after colors. Rubidius means "deepest red" in Latin, which is where rubidium got its name.

Praseodymium is a mouthful, but C. A. von Welsbach derived the name from a Greek word for "leek green."

Chemists love mythology. Promethium was named for Prometheus, a character from Greek mythology who stole fire from the gods to give to humans. Niobium was named for Niobe, another Greek mythological character. Thorium comes from the mighty Norse god Thor.

107   264
Bh
Bohrium

Score points back home! Where do you think germanium was discovered? Polonium was named by Marie Curie after Poland. Americium, californium, and berkelium were named by the same chemists at the University of California at Berkeley.

Holmium is named after Stockholm, Sweden. France has francium as well as gallium and lutetium, from the Roman names for France (Gaul) and Paris (Lutetia).

It's all politics: Element 104, discovered in 1964, remains stuck in controversy. Russian (then Soviet) scientists in

84   209
Po
Polonium

And the Winners Are . . .

Heaviest: element 118, over twice as heavy as chunky cesium

Lightest: hydrogen

Most common: hydrogen again. More than 90% of all the atoms in the universe are hydrogen.

Hardest: carbon in the form of a diamond.

Dubna claimed to have first synthesized 104 by blasting plutonium with neon ions. They called it kurchatovium after a Soviet physicist. But 1964 was the peak of the Cold War, and tensions between the U.S. and the then Soviet Union were extreme. A group of American scientists in Berkeley, California, claimed they invented it first and suggested calling it rutherfordium for a British physicist, Ernest Rutherford. Finally, IUPAC proposed that 104 be named unnilquadium—Latin for "one zero four." Nobody likes this idea.

79   196.09
Au
Gold

107   264
Bh
Bohrium

97   247
Bk
Berkelium

YOUR WORLD YOUR TURN

Final Project:
In Your Element

Scientists are creating elements all the time. Now it's your turn. Look at the periodic table for inspiration.

Working alone or with your classmates, pick any element on the periodic table. Be sure no two people pick the same one. Now thoroughly research this element. Learn everything you can about it, keeping these ideas in mind:

- Its uses, either by itself or in combination with other elements
- Its properties
- Its value to society
- Its monetary value
- How plentiful or scarce it is
- Where in the world it's found
- Its major claim to fame
- Where it got its name
- Its atomic structure

Write up all your findings any way you want—on index cards or paper, using sketches, photographs, diagrams. With your teacher's help and permission, post a giant-sized world map on the bulletin board or wall. Put everyone's elemental research on it and see the world transformed into a treasure chest.

Now be an advocate. Speak up for "your" element in a class debate. How could people get along without it? Which ecosystems depend on it? Could the world make better use of it? Is its monetary value appropriate to its worth? Look to the future: Will we always need or want the element in the same way we do now? Or will our wants and needs increase or decrease over time?

ANSWER Solve-It-Yourself Mystery, pages 22–23

The airship's tanks carried hydrogen, which burns. Wind knocked the airship into the landing mast, which poked a hole into the airship's skin, causing a hydrogen leak. The electrical charge in the atmosphere made a spark that caused the leaking gas to explode. Then the fabric caught fire. That's what the Naval Air Engineering Station at Lakehurst believes was the cause of the famous explosion of the Hindenburg, upon which this mystery was based. A NASA scientist, however, believes that lightning ignited an aluminum coating on the fabric. Give yourself points for any explanation that uses the clues logically and takes into account the nature of the elements that made up the ship and the conditions outside.